Famous People

NEIL ARMSTRONG
1930~

Christine Moorcroft

Magnus Magnusson

Christine Moorcroft is an educational consultant and an Ofsted inspector, who was a teacher in primary and special schools and a lecturer in education. She has written and edited several books on history and religion and on other subjects, including personal and social education, science and English.

Magnus Magnusson KBE, has written several books on history and archaeology, and translated many Icelandic sagas and modern Icelandic novels. He has presented major television programmes on history and archaeology, such as *Chronicle*, *The Archaeology of the Bible Lands* and *Living Legends*, as well as the long-running quiz series, *Mastermind*. He is currently chairman of Scottish Natural Heritage, the Government body which advises on environmental issues.

D1439552

ACKNOWLEDGEMENTS

The authors thank the following for their help: Doug Millard (Associate Curator for Space Technology, Science Museum, London), John Zwez (Curator: Neil Armstrong Museum [Ohio Historical Society], Wapakoneta, Ohio).

Picture credits
Ohio Historical Society: pages 4 (both), 5 (top), 7 (both), 10
NASA: pages 12 (bottom), 13, 14, 15 (both), 16, 17 (both), 18 (both), 19 (plaque)
Associated Press: 12 (top), 19 (flag)
Mary Evans Picture Library: page 5 (bottom)

Published by Channel Four Learning Limited
Castle House
75–76 Wells Street
London W1P 3RE

Written by Christine Moorcroft and Magnus Magnusson
Illustrated by Tony O'Donnell
Cover illustration by Jeffrey Burn
Designed by Blade Communications
Edited by Margot O'Keeffe
Printed by Alden Press
ISBN 1-86215-350-7

For further information about Channel 4 Schools
and details of published materials, contact
Channel 4 Schools
PO Box 100
Warwick CV34 6TZ
Tel: 01926 436444
Fax: 01926 436446

Contents

Growing up in Ohio

Neil Armstrong was born on 5 August 1930 in the United States of America. His father's job meant that the family had to move to live in many different towns in the state of Ohio.

When Neil was two years old, his father took him to the National Air Races at an airport near where they lived. From that day on Neil loved aeroplanes.

Just before he was six years old, his family moved to Warren, Ohio. By then he had a three-year-old sister, June, and a baby brother, Dean.

Above is a map of Ohio where Neil lived. Left:
1. Neil, at five years of age, with his sister, June.
2. Neil's home in Warren, Ohio.

When Neil was five, his father heard that a new aeroplane was coming to the airport. It was called the 'Tin Goose' because it was made from metal and shaped like a big flying goose. He took Neil to the airport, where they saw the plane on the runway.

Airports were much smaller then than they are now. People were allowed to go onto the runways to look at the planes. Neil and his father met one of the pilots. He took them for a short flight in the 'Tin Goose'.

Neil with his father and the 'Tin Goose'.

An advertisement for air travel in 1934.

WHILE YOU READ YOUR PAPER **AND HOME AGAIN**
THE SAME DAY!

NEARLY 1,700 PERSONS FLY BETWEEN LONDON & PARIS EVERY WEEK

The luxury of Imperial Airways' air liners is proverbial. Pullman-like comfort, meals, attentive stewards, lavatories and luggage space. For you, the chops of the Channel look like ripples and you arrive in Paris fresh and unfatigued, having spent no more time in the air than it takes to run your car from London to lunch with your cousins in the country. Air travel is not expensive and it is very delightful —try it!

LONDON TO PARIS
FROM . £4.15.0
RETURN . £7.12.0

PERIAL AIRWAYS

THE GREATEST AIR SERVICE IN THE WORLD

...n about Imperial Airways travel from the principal travel agents or from Airways Terminus, Victoria Station, S.W.1, or Imperial Airways ...harles Street, Lower Regent Street, S.W.1. Telephone : VICtoria 2211 (Day & Night). Telegrams : 'Impairlim, London.'

Did you know?

- In 1903, the first people flew in an aeroplane. They were Orville and Wilbur Wright, two brothers who built aeroplanes. They lived in Dayton, Ohio.

- By 1936, planes which carried up to 14 passengers had been built. They travelled at about 160 km per hour.

- At this time there were no jet engines.

Learning to fly

Neil read everything he could find about planes. He filled scrap-books with pictures and information about them. He spent hours making model planes which could fly.

When he was 11 years old he got a job mowing grass at a cemetery. He used some of the money to pay for aeroplane kits. Then he went to work at a bakery. By the time he was 13 he was building his own model planes from bits of wood, paper, straw, cardboard and anything else he could find.

Neil loved the thought of flying so much that he used to dream about it. In his dream he would hover above the ground if he held his breath. He did not quite fly, but nor did he fall to the ground.

In 1944 Neil went to Blume High School. He was in the Boy Scouts and learned how to make and follow maps and trails. He went camping and learned how to cook over a camp-fire. He also worked hard to earn his astronomy badge.

There were instructors at the local airport who gave flying lessons. Neil wanted to learn to fly. He was working in his spare time but he did not earn very much, so it took him a long time to save up the money for a flying lesson.

This is one of the model planes which Neil made when he was a boy.

Did you know?

- *Neil Armstrong had his first flying lesson when he was 15.*

- *He received his student pilot's licence on 5 August 1946, his 16th birthday.*

- *He got his pilot's licence before he passed his driving test.*

Neil's collection of books, maps and pictures about flying.

7

University and the Navy

Neil wanted to study aeroplanes and flying. But it cost a lot of money to go to the university and his parents could not afford it.

Then he found out that if he joined the Navy, he might get a scholarship which would pay for him to go to university. So he sent off an application form.

One day a letter came from the Navy. Neil had been awarded a scholarship. He was so happy! Now he could do what he had dreamed about all these years.

In 1950 most people thought it was impossible to get to the Moon.

After 18 months at university, Neil was sent by the Navy for flight training.

The Korean War started in June 1950 and Neil went there in 1951 on the aircraft carrier USS *Essex* with Fighter Squadron 51.

His task was to shoot at bridges, trains and tanks. It meant flying a Panther fighter jet very low, which was dangerous. On one of these flights, a shell hit a wing on his plane. Neil had to use the ejection seat and parachute to escape.

After Korea he left the Navy and went back to university.

The aircraft carrier, USS Essex, and two Panther jets, the aircraft Neil Armstrong flew in Korea.

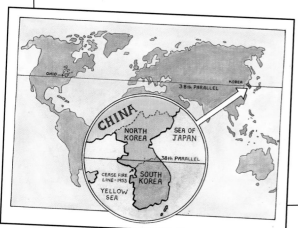

A map showing North and South Korea.

Did you know?

• Frank Whittle, an Englishman, had invented the jet engine in 1937. Jet planes could fly faster than the speed of sound – 1229 km per hour.

• North Korea invaded South Korea in 1950. In June, the United States began sending forces there.

• The war ended in 1953. There is a band of land between the two countries where no armies can go. It is called the 38th parallel.

Neil, the aviator

After university, Neil's first job was in Cleveland, Ohio, flying planes and doing research on rockets. Then he was sent to California to be a test-pilot, engineer and researcher.

Neil flew many different types of aircraft, including jets, helicopters and gliders. This was the best time of his life!

In January 1956 he married Janet Shearon, a girl he had met at university.

Neil married Janet Shearon in January 1956. They had met as students at Purdue University.

In 1960, Neil flew an *X-15* plane for the first time. He was the youngest person ever to fly one. It had a rocket engine and was launched from a *Boeing 52* jet. Altogether he flew it seven times. The highest he flew was 62,100 metres. The flights lasted only about ten minutes.

Later he said that the view from the *X-15* was like that from a spacecraft. He could see that the Earth was round. He said it was "fantastic."

From their home in the mountains Neil's wife, Janet, watched him through binoculars flying these aeroplanes.

Their son, Eric, was born in 1957, and their daughter, Karen, in 1959. In 1961 there was a sad time for the Armstrong family. Karen died from a brain tumour. She was only two years old.

Did you know?

- By 1935, German scientists were working on aircraft which used liquid rocket-fuel.

- In 1957, the USSR used a rocket to launch a satellite called Sputnik into space.

- On 12 April 1961 Yuri Gagarin from the USSR was the first human in space. He made one orbit of the Earth in Vostok 1.

Neil, the astronaut

Then two things happened to change Neil's life. John F Kennedy, the President of the United States of America, said that in the next ten years his country would send a man to the Moon and return him safely. Then in February 1962, a man named John Glenn orbited the Earth in *Mercury-Atlas 6*. He was one of the first seven astronauts in the country.

President John F Kennedy, who said that America would send men to the Moon.

Neil had been more interested in flying planes than spacecraft, but now he changed his mind. NASA was looking for the second team of astronauts. He applied to join them and was successful. In 1962 he began training on the *Gemini* spacecraft.

The first seven American astronauts. John Glenn is in the front row, second from the left.

In 1966, Neil went into space with David Scott. Their job was to link up with a satellite.

Neil carefully moved the nose of the spacecraft into position but then everything began to spin. The astronauts could not stop the spinning so they had to separate from the satellite.

The only thing to do was to end the mission and return to Earth. The astronauts were able to bring the spacecraft to a safe landing.

A ship rushed to their emergency landing place in the Pacific Ocean.

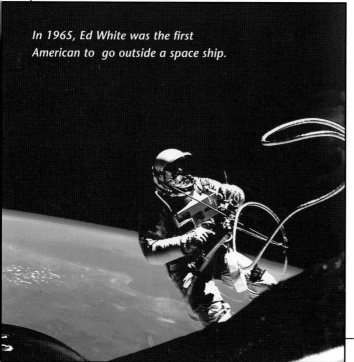

In 1965, Ed White was the first American to go outside a space ship.

Did you know?

- *At NASA people were finding ways to build better spacecraft to get people into space.*

- *Astronauts had to take not only food and water, but also air to breathe.*

- *Away from the pull of the Earth's gravity there is no 'up' or 'down'. Things (and people) float about in the air inside a spacecraft!*

Apollo

The first *Apollo* spacecraft to orbit the Moon was *Apollo 8*. A powerful rocket, *Saturn V*, was used to launch it into space on 21 December 1968.

The crew, Bill Anders, Frank Borman and Jim Lovell, sent back information about the surface of the Moon. Their journey back to Earth began on Christmas day. They opened some Christmas presents which they had taken with them!

The launch of Apollo 8 from Cape Kennedy, Florida, on 21 December 1968.

One of Neil's jobs to prepare for the Moon landing was to test the Lunar Landing Research Vehicle. It was called the 'Flying Bedstead' because of its funny shape and spindly legs.

During one test, in May 1968, the 'Flying Bedstead' went out of control. Neil tried to put things right, but he had to eject. He landed on the grass between the runways and the 'Flying Bedstead' crashed near the runway and burst into flames.

Above is a photograph of the Earth taken from Apollo 8 as it orbited the Moon. At the bottom of the picture is the surface of the Moon.

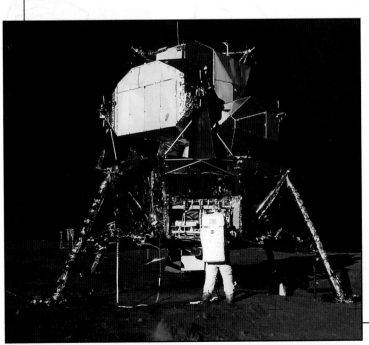

The Lunar Landing Research Vehicle.

Did you know?

- *Apollo 8 did not land on the Moon. It made ten orbits of the Moon and then returned to Earth.*

- *Apollo 9 and Apollo 10 astronauts tested the spacecraft. But still no astronaut had landed on the Moon.*

The Moon

On 16 July 1969, *Apollo 11* stood on the launch pad at Cape Kennedy. It was going to take three men to the Moon. Neil Armstrong was the flight commander, and with him were Edwin 'Buzz' Aldrin and Michael Collins. A *Saturn V* rocket launched *Apollo 11* into space.

It took three days to reach the Moon. Now for the landing! Michael Collins stayed in the *Apollo 11* command module, *Columbia*, orbiting the Moon. Neil Armstrong and Buzz Aldrin were in *Eagle*, the landing module. They lowered *Eagle*'s legs, checked all its systems and then separated it from *Apollo*. Several hours later they were flying over the Moon.

Neil Armstrong was appointed as flight commander to Apollo 11.

The Eagle and Neil Armstrong on the Moon.

Back on Earth this message was heard. "Houston, Tranquillity Base here. The *Eagle* has landed."

They had done it! Neil Armstrong and Buzz Aldrin were on the Moon! They grinned at one another from inside their helmets. Now they were ready to explore.

They opened the hatch and lowered the ladder. Then Neil climbed down and stepped onto the firm but dusty ground.

What he said next has become famous: "That's one small step for a man...one giant leap for mankind."

Eagle rejoining Columbia, 110 km above the Moon. Once Armstrong and Aldrin were on back on board, Eagle was left behind. It was no longer needed.

Did you know?

- *Neil Armstrong and Buzz Aldrin had a list of jobs to do on the Moon.*

- *They set up a television camera, collected samples of rock and took photographs.*

- *They described what they saw to the people watching on Earth.*

- *They spent 2 hours 31 minutes on the Moon outside Eagle.*

Back on Earth

Millions of people watched their television screens. In the Pacific Ocean, the crew of USS *Hornet* waited. Some of them looked at the sky. At home, Neil's family waited.

A dot was seen in the sky. Then a small dark cone floated out of the clouds on three orange and white striped parachutes. It was *Columbia*, the command module of *Apollo 11*. It splashed down into the sea and air filled the big airbags to make it turn the right way up.

Above: Divers put a collar filled with air around Columbia to keep it afloat.

Neil Armstrong, Michael Collins and Buzz Aldrin in their special trailer. President Nixon is outside, welcoming them back to Earth.

Everybody celebrated the landing on the Moon. The astronauts met presidents, kings and queens of countries around the world.

Neil did not go into space again. He worked for NASA until 1971, then became a professor of aerospace engineering at the University of Cincinnati.

A big parade in New York welcomed the astronauts back.

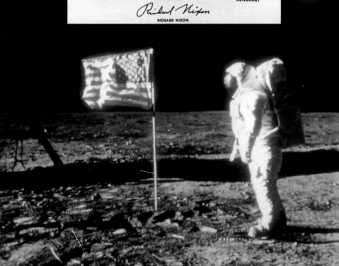

The astronauts put up the American flag and left this plaque on the Moon.

Did you know?

- Scientists thought there was no life on the Moon, but they were not sure. There might have been some germs which could live without air or water. Since then, water has been found on the Moon.

- The astronauts had to stay in quarantine for three weeks to make sure they had not brought back any germs.

Time-lines

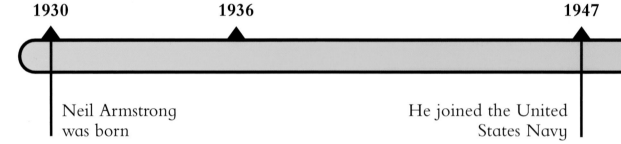

He went on
his first flight

1930   **1936**   **1947**

Neil Armstrong
was born

He joined the United
States Navy

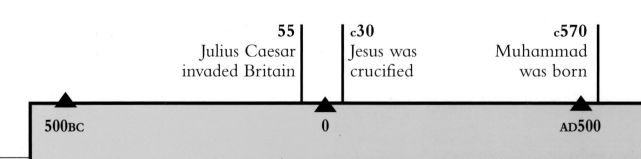

55
Julius Caesar
invaded Britain

c30
Jesus was
crucified

c570
Muhammad
was born

500BC   0   AD**500**

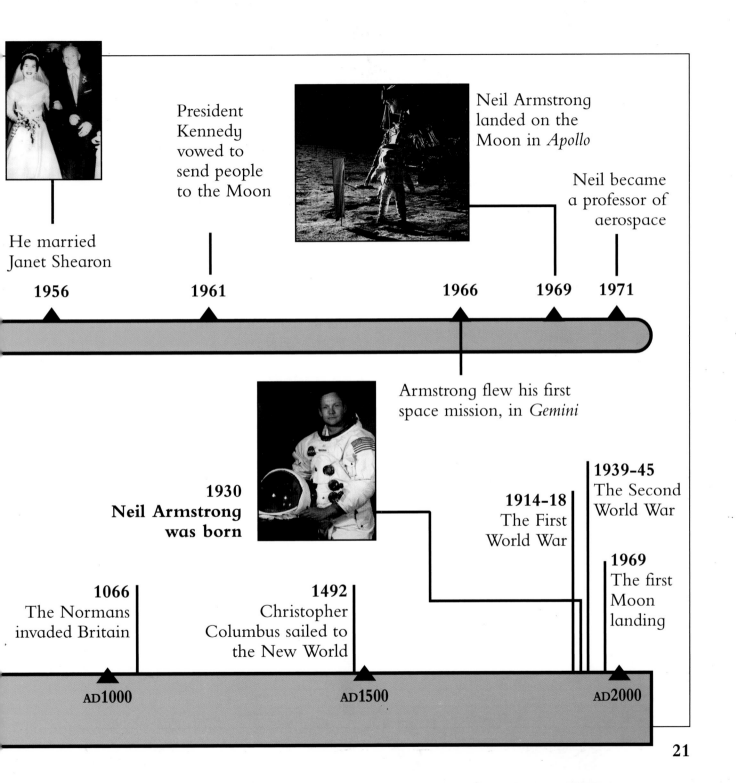

He married
Janet Shearon

1956

President
Kennedy
vowed to
send people
to the Moon

1961

Neil Armstrong
landed on the
Moon in *Apollo*

Neil became
a professor of
aerospace

1966   **1969**   **1971**

Armstrong flew his first
space mission, in *Gemini*

1930
**Neil Armstrong
was born**

1939–45
The Second
World War

1914–18
The First
World War

1969
The first
Moon
landing

1066
The Normans
invaded Britain

1492
Christopher
Columbus sailed to
the New World

AD1000   AD1500   AD2000

How to find out more

More books to read

Neil Armstrong, Young Flyer by Montrew Dunham (Aladdin, 1996)

Gagarin and Armstrong by Clint Twist (Evans, 1995)

Twenty Names in Space Exploration by Brian Williams (Wayland, 1989)

The Universe by James Muirden (Kingfisher, 1986)

Sun, Moon and Planets by Lynn Myring & Sheila Snowden (Usborne, 1982)

Rockets and Spacecraft by Lynn Myring (Usborne, 1982)

Our Earth by Jane Chisholm (Usborne, 1982)

Television programmes to watch

Channel 4 Schools series, Stop Look, Listen: Famous People. Telephone 01926 436444.

Newspapers

Daily Telegraph 3 January, 1956
Evening News 21 July, 1969
Daily Telegraph 21 July, 1969
Daily Mail 9 April, 1994

Places to visit or to which to write

Liverpool Planetarium,
William Brown Street,
Liverpool L3 8EN.
Tel 0151 207 0001

London Planetarium,
Marylebone Road,
London NW1 5LR.
Tel 0171 935 6861

Neil Armstrong Air and Space Museum,
Wapakoneta, Ohio.

Newcastle Discovery Museum,
Blandford Square,
Newcastle Upon Tyne NE1 4JL.
Tel 0191 232 6789.

Ohio Historical Society
1985 Velma Avenue
Columbus
Ohio.

Science Museum (Exploration of Space Gallery),
Exhibition Road
London SW7 2DD.
Tel 0171 938 9000.

Glossary

aerospace engineering *(19)* Making aircraft and spacecraft.

application *(8)* A form or letter written to ask for a place on a course or a job.

astronaut *(12)* Someone who flies spacecraft.

astronomy *(7)* The study of stars.

aviator *(10)* Someone who flies aeroplanes.

ejection *(9)* Being pushed out of a plane for safety.

engineer *(10)* Someone who designs and makes engines and machines.

glider *(10)* A plane which flies without an engine.

gravity *(13)* The force which pulls things towards the Earth (or another planet, moon or star).

jet engine *(5)* An engine which moves a plane forwards by pushing gases in the opposite direction.

module *(16)* Part of a spacecraft which can be separated from the rest, for example, for landing.

NASA *(12)* National Aeronautics and Space Administration (in the USA).

orbit *(11)* The path followed by something which travels round a planet, star or moon.

researcher *(10)* Someone who finds things out by investigating, experimenting and reading.

satellite *(11)* Something which orbits the Earth (or a planet, star or moon).

scholarship *(8)* Money paid for a student to study.

squadron *(9)* A group of aeroplanes.

test-pilot *(10)* A pilot whose job is to try out aircraft.

Tranquillity *(17)* The Sea of Tranquillity is an area of the Moon. It is a flat stretch of dusty land.

X-15 *(11)* A very fast jet plane.

Index